WARSHIPS

MARK DARTFORD

Lerner Publications Company
Minneapolis

First American edition published by Lerner Publications Company.

Copyright © 2003 by The Brown Reference Group plc.

Lerner Publications Company.
A division of Lerner Publishing Group
241 First Avenue North
Minneapolis, MN55401 U.S.A.

Website address: www.lernerbooks.com

Library of Congress Cataloging-in-Publication Data

Dartford, Mark.
 Warships / by Geoff Cornish.
       p. cm. -- (Military hardware in action)
Includes index.
Summary: Profiles some of the different warships used by the
United States Navy and other navies around the world, describing their
design, weapons, and uses.
  ISBN 0–8225–4703–1 (lib. bdg.)
1. Warships--Juvenile literature. [1. Warships.] I. Title. II.
Series.
  V7506.D37 2003
  359.8'3--dc21   2002013599

Printed in China
Bound in the United States of America
1 2 3 4 5 6 – OS – 08 07 06 05 04 03

This book uses black and yellow chevrons as a decorative element on some headers. They do not point to other elements on the page.

Contents

Introduction

A sleek **destroyer** gently pushes through the choppy waves of a swelling ocean. Without warning, light and smoke burst from the ship's deck. A missile streaks upward into the sky. Beyond the horizon, a target will soon be hit.

LAUNCH

An anti-aircraft missile fires from a destroyer sailing with two companions.

>> **destroyer** – a fast, medium-sized warship often used to escort carriers

Wooden World

Navies have fought battles at sea for hundreds of years. Until the 1800s, ships were made of wood and had canvas sails. Rows of cannons fired iron balls or iron fragments to shatter enemy **hulls** or to rip their sails.

ANCIENT CLASHES

Greek and Persian ships at the Battle of Salamis (480 B.C.), the first recorded full-scale naval battle in history. Slaves provided the muscle power to propel these long vessels at speeds up to 25 miles per hour. The ancient Persians, Greeks, and Romans all used warships to attack and defend their empires.

GREAT AGE OF SAIL

During the American Revolution (1775–1783), the American *Bonhomme Richard* (*left*) and HMS *Serapis* (*right*) clashed off northern England on September 23, 1779. The British put a hole in the American ship, which began to sink. Its captain, John Paul Jones, refused to surrender and declared "I have not yet begun to fight." Instead, he forced the British ship to surrender before the *Bonhomme Richard* sank.

Iron and Steam

The mid-1800s was a time of technical improvements for warfare at sea. Wind power gave way to steam power. Mighty ironclads (armor-plated vessels) replaced the fragile wooden ships of earlier times.

MERRIMACK AND MONITOR

During the Civil War (1861–1865), the Confederate ironclad *Merrimack* (*left*) met its Union match, the *Monitor* (*right*), at Hampton Roads, Virginia. The two ships slugged it out for more than three hours. But neither could do much damage to the other. The battle ended in a draw.

World Wars

World War I (1914–1918) and World War II (1939–1945) greatly sped up the development of warships. Huge battleships became symbols of a country's military strength.

ESCORT DUTY

The battleship USS *New Jersey* in 1918. Most U.S. warships in World War I were used to protect the Atlantic **convoys** that carried supplies and troops to the battlefields in Europe.

OCEAN BATTLEFIELDS

The USS *Nevada* bombarded the Japanese-held island of Iwo Jima in 1945. In World War II, the navies of the leading combatant countries fought each other across most of the world's oceans.

Postwar Changes

After World War II, the world's most powerful countries—the United States and the Soviet Union—built larger navies with more types of ships. Heavy battleships were less important than aircraft carriers. Smaller **escorts** acted as defensive and attacking forces.

Warship Categories

The main fighting ships of the world's naval forces are divided into three main categories. Each category—cruisers, destroyers, and frigates—relates to the size of the ships. **Classes** of ships are within each category. The ships in each class share the same design. Most battle groups are made up of these various warships. They are often under the command of an aircraft carrier. Many other service craft also provide support and maintenance for these fighting ships.

CRUISERS

A Ticonderoga class **guided missile cruiser** turns at high speed. Cruisers are usually larger than other warships, except for aircraft carriers. Cruisers displace (move aside) more than 10,000 tons of water. They carry a wide range of weapons and can take on several missions at a time.

DESTROYERS

A U.S. Navy guided missile destroyer. Destroyers are fast warships that are often used to protect larger battle groups. They are medium-sized warships that displace 5,000 to 10,000 tons of water.

FRIGATES

The guided missile frigate USS *Kauffman* pushes through the Atlantic Ocean. Frigates are the smallest class of fighting ship. They usually displace between 2,000 and 5,000 tons of water. Frigates generally have a single task, such as anti-submarine warfare (ASW). The U.S. Navy is replacing frigates with cruisers and destroyers.

The Cruiser's Job

Cruisers are the U.S. Navy's traditional big-hitters. They evolved from battleships and battle cruisers. These were the most important fighting ships in the fleet until aircraft carriers took over. Cruisers are equipped with long-range weapons and high-tech sensor equipment. These tools make them powerful in both defense and attack.

BATTLESHIPS

The USS *New Jersey* was the last Iowa class battleship. It was the largest, fastest, and most powerful U.S. battleship ever built. Guided missile cruisers have replaced most battleships and battle cruisers. Cruisers are smaller but pack a bigger punch. All three have played a major part in policing the world's oceans.

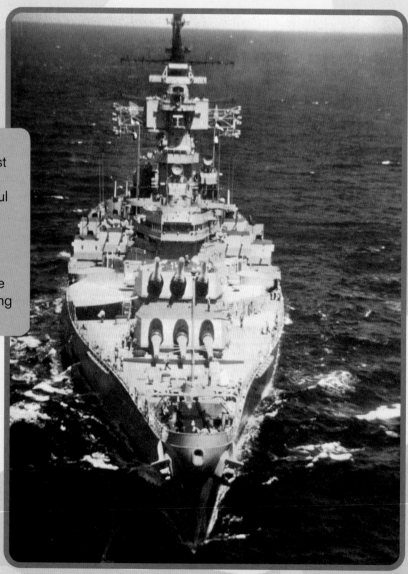

NUCLEAR CRUISERS

The nuclear-powered guided missile cruiser USS *Mississippi* has almost unlimited range. Cruisers often act as extra muscle power in a large **carrier group** but can also operate on their own.

CRUISE MISSILES

Some U.S. Navy guided missile cruisers are equipped with Tomahawk cruise missiles. These are long-range missiles intended to strike targets on land. Cruisers with cruise missiles have a **strategic** role, since they can hit very hard from far away.

The Cruiser's Job

Cruisers can do several jobs. They have a powerful strategic capability when equipped with cruise missiles. They also operate as **reconnaissance** and **surveillance** craft. Cruisers also hunt for enemy submarines and shoot down enemy aircraft.

USS *LAKE ERIE*

The guided missile cruiser USS *Lake Erie* glides on a calm, gray ocean. This is a Ticonderoga class cruiser, equipped with the Aegis radar system. Aegis is so sophisticated it can find attacking missiles over the horizon. It can also guide anti-missile missiles toward them.

>> **reconnaissance** – approaching enemy positions to observe their

Battle Force

U.S. Navy guided missile cruisers perform mainly in a battle force role. They are multimission surface ships that support carrier groups and amphibious (land and sea) task forces. Cruisers are officially described as "Battle Force Capable," which means that they have many combat roles.

USS *LONG BEACH*

The nuclear-powered USS *Long Beach* is a Battle Force Capable guided missile cruiser that can fight independently of a battle group.

FRIENDS AT SEA

A cruiser supply ship sits alongside the nuclear-powered guided missile cruiser USS *Leahy. Leahy* has almost unlimited fuel, but it still needs other supplies. By bringing the supplies out to sea, the U.S. Navy can keep its main fighting ships where they are most needed.

Greyhounds

Destroyers, because they are so fast, have been described as "greyhounds of the sea." Destroyers first appeared at the end of the 1800s. Their purpose was to destroy a new kind of fast **torpedo boat** that could threaten larger ships. Although destroyers have changed greatly, they remain fast compared to other fighting ships. They also continue to protect larger ships.

ASW ROLE

The ASW destroyer USS *Spruance* sails in the Atlantic. ASW destroyers protect other ships from submarine attack. *Spruance* carries SH60 Sea Hawk helicopters for submarine surveillance and attack.

FAST AND FURIOUS

The guided missile destroyer USS *Arleigh Burke* runs at full speed. The Arleigh Burke class has similar capability to the Ticonderoga class cruisers. In fact, guided missile destroyers are really small-scale versions of the guided missile cruisers. The Arleigh Burke class combines missile power with anti-aircraft and ASW fleet protection tasks.

ESCORT DUTIES

A French navy destroyer *(left)* escorts the USS *Passumpsic* as it refuels the aircraft carrier USS *Ranger (right)*. The destroyer's job is to protect the fuel tender, or supply ship, and the carrier during this risky operation.

Frigates

Frigates are low-cost warships. They are smaller than cruisers and destroyers. They do not have the same all-around capability. Most U.S. Navy frigates have either anti-submarine or anti-aircraft roles. Like ASW destroyers, some frigates also carry submarine-hunter helicopters. Frigates are solidly built. They can sustain much damage and still be repaired.

PERRY CLASS

The Oliver Hazard Perry class guided missile frigate USS *Ford* participates in **sea trials**. More than 30 Perry class frigates are in U.S. Navy service. Most of them are tasked with protection of shipping (POS) duties.

Command Ships Escort

The Seventh **Fleet Command Ship**, USS *Blue Ridge*, is escorted by the guided missile cruiser USS *Sterrett (left)* and the guided missile frigate USS *Rodney M. Davis (right)*. Although small, frigates are quick and easy to move around. This makes them a useful source of protection for larger ships.

AIR POWER

An SH2 Sea Sprite lands on the helicopter pad aboard the ASW destroyer USS *Nicholson*. Helicopters provide the added range needed to find submarines before they can strike. The helicopters also carry the weapons to prevent the attacks.

Warship Weapons

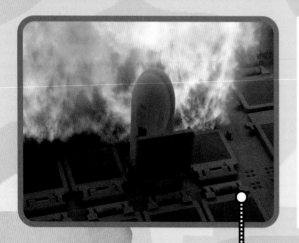

Fighting ships are equipped with many defensive and offensive weapons. These include surface-to-surface missiles, surface-to-air missiles, and rockets. The ships also carry guns of different **calibers**, torpedoes, mines, and aircraft.

TOMAHAWK

A Tomahawk cruise missile leaps in a sea of flames from its launch **silo** on the guided missile destroyer USS *Fife* during Operation Desert Storm in 1991. Tomahawk missiles are carried on some classes of cruiser and destroyer. Tomahawks, which can carry nuclear weapons, are the hardest hitting and longest-range missiles in the U.S. Navy.

HARPOON

An RGM84 Harpoon missile shoots out of its canister launcher aboard the USS *Leahy*. Harpoons can be used against air, sea, or land targets and have a range of up to 150 miles.

STANDARD

An RIM67 Standard surface-to-air missile fires from the guided missile destroyer USS *Gainsborough*. Standards are the navy's main medium-range anti-aircraft missile. They can bring down airplanes up to 100 miles away.

TORPEDO

A Mark 46 torpedo launches from the deck tube of a U.S. Navy guided missile destroyer. The Mk46 is designed to attack high performance submarines. It is the main torpedo used by the forces of the North Atlantic Treaty Organization (NATO), a defensive alliance. The Mk46 can be launched from ships, submarines, helicopters, or airplanes. It can also be fitted with anti-submarine rockets (ASROCs).

Gunnery

Guns have played a key role in combat at sea from the earliest days. Although modern warships rely increasingly on missile technology, nearly all fighting ships have guns for close-in defense and attack.

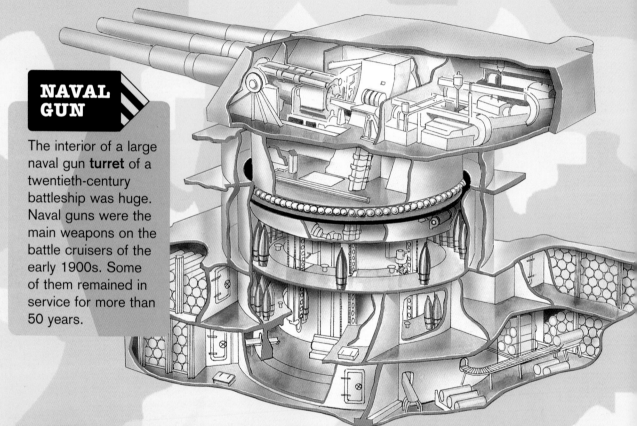

NAVAL GUN

The interior of a large naval gun **turret** of a twentieth-century battleship was huge. Naval guns were the main weapons on the battle cruisers of the early 1900s. Some of them remained in service for more than 50 years.

DECK GUN

A crewmember inspects the 76mm foredeck gun on the U.S. Navy frigate USS *Halyburton*. Sea spray and the effects of rough weather can damage the controls of such sophisticated weapons.

Close-in Defense

A Phalanx automatic gun is mounted on the deck of a U.S. Navy cruiser. Phalanx is a radar-controlled close-in anti-aircraft system. The **radar dish** below the gun port finds approaching aircraft and automatically directs a stream of high-speed 20mm shells toward them.

ON THE RAILS

A crewmember tests a 25mm gun fitted to the deckrail of the USS *Antietam*. Because the gun is not permanently fixed and armor plated, it is protected by a wall of sandbags placed around it.

Warships in Action

Battles at sea are as old as warfare itself. Warship technology has progressed dramatically from the days of timber and sail. But a warship's fighting role has changed very little. It is still meant to defend national territories by extending a line of defense out into the sea.

World War I

BATTLE OF JUTLAND

In May 1916, the British Royal Navy and the German Imperial Fleet clashed in the Battle of Jutland in the North Sea. It was the only major sea battle of World War I. The German commander, Admiral Scheer, tried to lure British battle cruisers and destroyers into a trap. However, British **codebreakers** intercepted German signals. The British commander, Admiral Jellicoe, set his own countertrap.

>> **codebreaker** – a person who figures out secret enemy messages

World War II

During World War II, as many decisive battles took place at sea as on land. In the early stages of the war, sea warfare was mainly confined to convoy routes across the Atlantic Ocean and the Mediterranean Sea. Naval actions there and in the Pacific shaped the course of the war.

ATLANTIC CONVOYS

Crewmembers from the USS *Arkansas* monitor a group of convoy ships in the mid Atlantic in 1942. The supply route between North America and Europe was vital to the Allied war effort. It was also a tempting target for German **U-boats**. They were intent on sinking the slow cargo vessels.

MEDITERRANEAN TURMOIL

An Italian cruiser fights during the Battle of Matapan in 1941. In the Mediterranean Sea, a small force of British warships challenged the enemy navy's cruisers and destroyers. The Italian ships were threatening convoys in the Mediterranean. Several Italian cruisers sank, and the Italian navy retreated to port for the rest of the war.

Warships in Action

Japan declared war on the United States following its surprise attack on Pearl Harbor in the Hawaiian Islands in 1941. From this date, many of the most important sea and air battles of World War II took place in the Pacific Ocean.

Pacific Warfare

THUNDERBOLT

The USS *Arizona* burns fiercely after being hit by a Japanese bomb at Pearl Harbor. The Japanese attacked the U.S. base on the island of Oahu on December 7, 1941. Japanese aircraft sank or damaged 18 U.S. warships.

LEYTE GULF

Bombs dropped from a U.S. **B25** bomber hit a Japanese destroyer during the battle for Leyte Gulf in the Philippines in October 1944. Described as the greatest sea battle of all, Leyte Gulf marked the beginning of the end for the Japanese navy. U.S. forces sank a total of 26 ships but lost only 6 of their own ships.

DEVASTATION

"Our force entered Pearl to witness a ghastly sight of sunken ships—oil covered water—and ruins. We first passed the *Nevada* which had been beached to prevent sinking. Next was *California*—badly damaged and on the bottom. The hull of the *Oklahoma* then came in sight after having capsized.... The *Arizona* was completely blown up and a twisted mass of iron.... It was a sight none of us like to remember but must avenge!"

Radioman 1st Class Raymond M. Tuftland, U.S. Navy, December 1941

Korean War

CUTTING THE SUPPLY LINES

The battle cruiser USS *Missouri* unleashes a **salvo** of 16-inch shells against North Korean shore positions during the Korean War (1950–1953). A sea invasion later cut North Korean supply lines.

Warships in Action

The Middle East has been an international trouble spot for many years. U.S. and international naval forces patrol the oceans to try to maintain peace in the region.

DESERT STRIKE

A Tomahawk cruise missile is launched against Iraq from the **foredeck** of the guided missile cruiser USS *Shiloh* in September 1996. The missiles were reinforcing the **no-fly zone** imposed on Iraq after Operation Desert Storm (1991).

ENDURING FREEDOM

The guided missile destroyer USS *O'Kane* patrols the Persian Gulf as part of Operation Enduring Freedom. Enduring Freedom was the international, U.S.-led response to terrorist attacks in the United States in September 2001.

STRIKE BACK

The guided missile cruiser USS *Philippine Sea* launches a long-range cruise missile against terrorist hideouts in Afghanistan. Although far inland, these targets can still be accurately pinpointed from the ocean.

>> **no-fly zone** = an area where military flying is prohibited

Life Aboard

A warship is a fighting machine, but it is also a home for its crewmembers. Each person has special skills that together make an effective fighting force. The number of crewmembers depends on the size of the ship. A small frigate may accommodate about 12 officers and 300 **enlisted** crew. A large cruiser may carry 50 officers and 800 enlisted crew.

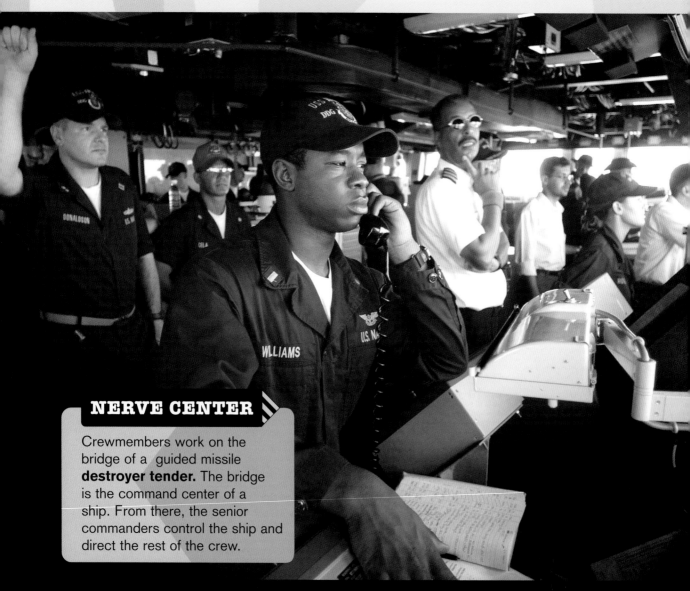

NERVE CENTER

Crewmembers work on the bridge of a guided missile **destroyer tender.** The bridge is the command center of a ship. From there, the senior commanders control the ship and direct the rest of the crew.

>> **enlisted** – men or women who are not officers

FORMAL DAYS

Sailors stand at attention aboard the guided missile destroyer USS *Shoup*. Formal occasions when full dress uniforms are worn are very much a part of military life. The discipline required during ceremonial duties reflects the discipline needed to stay calm and to follow orders in combat.

INFORMAL DAYS

Crewmembers of the destroyer tender USS *Yellowstone* take time out for a dockside barbecue during Operation Desert Storm. Crewmembers are encouraged to make good use of their free time while in port overseas. They are also asked to remember that they are representing their nation.

Life Aboard

A ship's **complement** is divided into different sections, or crews, according to the type of work done. These include deck crews, weapons crews, engine crews, and communications crews. Support personnel include cooks and medical staff.

ON THE DECK

The deck department crewmembers aboard the destroyer USS *Fife* operate an anchor chain. In rough seas and freezing winds, jobs like this become difficult and dangerous. Protective clothing is essential.

TALKING FLAGS

A signaler aboard the guided missile cruiser USS *South Carolina* uses **semaphore** to communicate with another ship. Radio or other electronic surveillance can't find this simple form of signaling. The signaler must also have the skills required to operate complicated satellite communications equipment.

STANDING WATCH

A sailor in the bow of the guided missile frigate USS *Robert G. Bradley* watches for mines during operations in the Persian Gulf. Keeping a constant lookout is a feature of life at sea that goes back to the earliest days of sail. Even a ship crammed with space-age electronics relies on the human eye to spot unusual objects in the water.

Life Aboard

Taking a job at sea is very different from taking a job on land. Life onboard means constant movement, small spaces, and the same faces, even after work. The challenges are often more demanding but also more satisfying. Being prepared for combat at sea demands that little bit extra.

READY FOR ACTION

U.S. Navy **SEAL**s climb down a rope ladder into an inflatable boat, ready to board a suspicious vessel. SEALs are an elite force. They are trained for undercover operations and **close-quarter combat** on land, at sea, and in the air. SEALs can join the company of any vessel likely to get close to the enemy.

>> **SEAL** – abbreviation for Sea/Air/Land Special Forces troops

WELCOME HOME

Family and friends gather to welcome home the crew of a U.S. Navy warship from a mission in the Middle East. After months at sea, being reunited with loved ones is a rewarding moment.

RESPONSIBLE CAREER

"Sometimes it's scary to be responsible for so many people (we have over 600 sailors and marines on the ship right now). You get used to it, though, and I actually enjoy it!... You take on more responsibility, more equipment, and larger numbers of people as you become more senior."

Lieutenant Commander Sheila Scarborough,
Executive Officer, USS *Fort McHenry*

Warship Enemies

Warships are slow, compared to airplanes. Warships are large and easy to see, compared to a tank. In an open ocean, there is no natural cover to hide a warship. Warships seem like easy targets for attack by submarines, surface ships, or aircraft. But they have good defenses as well.

AIR ATTACK

Swooping down from the clouds, an F14 *(right)* and an F/A18 *(left)* armed with bombs and missiles can sink a warship in minutes. Most warships can find approaching aircraft on their radar. They take defensive action before the attackers get within range.

SURFACE ATTACK

Ship-launched surface-to-surface missiles can skim the ocean surface. They fly just a few feet above the waves. This makes them very hard to find or to knock out.

MISSILE HIT

The British destroyer HMS *Sheffield* was struck by an Argentine **Exocet missile** during the 1982 Falklands War. Exocet was designed as a surface-to-surface missile. The Argentine navy adapted it for launch by long-range Super Etendard strike aircraft. The *Sheffield* caught fire and had to be **scuttled**.

>> **scuttle** = to deliberately sink a ship, especially by its own crew

Warship Enemies

Warships are also at risk of attack from beneath the water. Mines, torpedoes, and submarines can all be ready to strike.

SUBMARINE

Hunter-killer submarines attack swiftly and with deadly effect. They are armed with torpedoes and missiles that can be launched underwater and are a warship's most dangerous hidden enemy.

UNSEEN DANGER

The U.S. Navy uses a range of torpedoes. Some of these can be launched by aircraft or ships, as well as from a submarine. Torpedoes are self-propelled, with quiet electric motors that make little sound in the water.

Modern U.S. Navy Torpedoes

Mk 44

Mk 46

Mk 50

Hitting Back

Warships are equipped with many defenses against air and sea attack. They often sail in groups to combine their defensive power.

ANTI-AIRCRAFT MISSILES

An **ordnance** crew loads a Sea Sparrow anti-aircraft missile into its launcher aboard a U.S. Navy warship. Sea Sparrow is a radar-guided weapon that can attack aircraft or missiles from any direction. Sea Sparrow is fitted to most U.S. Navy and NATO warships.

ANTI-SUBMARINE WARFARE

A destroyer-based Sea Sprite ASW helicopter hovers. These helicopters carry sonar underwater listening equipment to find enemy submarines. They can also attack by dropping **depth charges** or by firing missiles and rockets.

Warships

Destroyers, cruisers, and frigates act as the eyes, ears, and watchdogs of the fleet. Each class offers something different.

USS *TICONDEROGA*

The USS *Ticonderoga* sails through the Suez Canal en route to a mission in the Arabian Sea. The Ticonderoga class of guided missile cruisers was originally developed as destroyers but was redesignated in 1980. Ticonderogas are equipped with the Aegis air defense system, which is the most advanced of its kind in the world.

Details:
Crew: 24 officers, 340 enlisted
Length: 567 ft.
Beam: 55 ft.
Propulsion: 4 x 80,000 hp gas **turbines**, 2 shafts
Max Speed: 30 kts.
Displacement: 9,957 tons
Aircraft: 4 helicopters

USS *ARLEIGH BURKE*

The USS *Arleigh Burke* makes headway in a calm sea. The Arleigh Burke class of destroyers is the U.S. Navy's most capable and robust fighting ship. It is equipped with the Aegis air defense system. It also has the world's most advanced ASW technology.

Details:
Crew: 23 officers, 300 enlisted
Length: 505 ft.
Beam: 66 ft.
Propulsion: 4 x 100,000 hp gas turbines, 2 shafts
Max Speed: 31 kts.
Displacement: 8,300 tons
Aircraft: landing deck available

USS *DOYLE*

The Oliver Hazard Perry class ship USS *Doyle* sails in calm waters. The Perry class of guided missile frigates is the only remaining frigate class in the U.S. Navy. They have been upgraded to serve well into the twenty-first century. Their main job is to protect other fleet or carrier group ships from submarine attack.

Details:
Crew: 13 officers, 287 enlisted
Length: 453 ft.
Beam: 45 ft.
Propulsion: 2 x gas turbines, 41,000 hp total, 1 shaft
Max Speed: 29 kts.
Displacement: 4,100 tons
Aircraft: 1–2 helicopters

Warships

Most small to medium-sized warships have defensive roles. Their job is usually to protect the larger aircraft carriers and **amphibious assault ships** that make up the striking force of a fleet or task group at sea.

HMCS *OTTAWA*

HMCS *Ottawa* sails off the coast of Canada. The Canadian navy's Halifax class of frigates is built in Canada to match the country's need for ships that can operate at high speeds in rough seas and at very low temperatures.

Details:
Crew: 17 officers, 180 enlisted
Length: 441 ft. 9 in.
Beam: 53 ft. 8 in.
Propulsion: 2 x gas turbines, 47,494 hp, 2 shafts
Max Speed: 29 kts.
Displacement: 4,770 tons
Aircraft: 1 helicopter

>> **amphibious assault ship** – a ship that carries troops, armor, and aircraft

HMS *MANCHESTER*

HMS *Manchester* speeds through the Atlantic. *Manchester* is a British Type 42 destroyer. Type 42s are the backbone of the Royal Navy's air defense capability. They are equipped with Sea Dart anti-aircraft missiles that can also be used against surface vessels.

Details:
Crew: 31 officers, 270 enlisted
Length: 462 ft. 9 in.
Beam: 49 ft.
Propulsion: 2 x gas turbines, 54,450 hp total, 2 shafts
Max Speed: 29 kts.
Displacement: 4,675 tons
Aircraft: 1 helicopter

USS *KIDD*

The USS *Kidd* heads up the Kidd class of destroyers. They are the most powerful multipurpose destroyers in the U.S. Navy fleet. There are four Kidd guided missile destroyers. All are based on the Spruance hull design but have upgraded weapons systems. Some of these ships have been loaned to friendly foreign navies.

Details:
Crew: 40 officers, 340 enlisted
Length: 563 ft.
Beam: 55 ft.
Propulsion: 4 x gas turbines, total 80,000 hp, 2 shafts
Max Speed: 33 kts.
Displacement: 9,783 tons
Aircraft: 1–2 helicopters

Future Warships

Future warships will be quieter and **stealthier**. They will make more use of technology, and they will have more accurate weapons systems. Many will be able to combine several different roles at one time.

ASSAULT SHIP

An illustration shows the LPD-17, the first in a new class of U.S. Navy amphibious assault ships. These ships will greatly improve the ability of the Navy and U.S. Marine Corps to fight overseas.

ction systems

FUTURE COMBAT

An illustration shows the idea of a Future Surface Combatant (FSC). The United States and other countries are developing FSC to replace current destroyer fleets.

HSV

The U.S. Navy High Speed Vessel (HSV) Experimental Craft performed sea trials in the Arabian Sea during Operation Enduring Freedom. Its **trimaran** hull is built for speed. The craft is currently being used for rapid troop transport. There are also plans to develop larger warships using the same technology and design.

>> **trimaran** – a three-section hull that gives speed and stability

Future Warships

Warships are expensive to build, so **modular construction** techniques will play a major part in future warship design. This means that some types of ship, often shared between several countries, will have parts in common such as hulls and weapons systems.

Type 45 Destroyer

The British Royal Navy is developing a new generation of destroyers to replace its Type 42. These new destroyers will have a mainly anti-aircraft role, with new long-range radar detection equipment.

>> **modular construction** – assembled using prefabricated parts

Zumwalt Class Destroyer

Zumwalt is the name given to the new DD21 class of destroyer. This new generation of warships will be faster, harder to find, and easier to maintain than the ships they will replace. The class is named in honor of Admiral Elmo Zumwalt Jr., the U.S. Navy's chief of operations from 1970 to 1974.

SWIFT AND SILENT

Described as **land attack destroyers**, the Zumwalt class of ships will replace current destroyers and frigates in the U.S. Navy fleet. They will have a low-lying stealthy design. Engines and power will all be electric, driven by the new Integrated Power System (IPS).

Hardware at a Glance

AA = anti-aircraft
ASROC = anti-submarine rocket
ASW = anti-submarine warfare
DD21 = Zumwalt class destroyer
HMCS = Her/His Majesty's Canadian Ship
HMS = Her/His Majesty's Ship
HSV = High Speed Vessel
IPS = Integrated Power System

NATO = North Atlantic Treaty Organization
POS = protection of shipping
SEAL = Sea/Air/Land Special Forces
U-boat = German submarine
USS = United States Ship

Further Reading & Websites

Bartlett, Richard. *United States Navy.* New York: Heinemann Library, 2003.

Chant, Christopher. *The History of the World's Warships.* New York: Book Sales, 2000.

Delgado, James P. *Wrecks of American Warships.* London: Franklin Watts, 2000.

Faulkner, Keith. *Jane's Warship Recognition Guide.* New York: HarperResource, 1999.

Gaines, Ann Graham. *The Navy in Action.* Berkeley Heights, NJ: Enslow Publishing, 2001.

Grant, George. *Warships: from the Galley to the Present Day.* New York: Gramercy, 2001.

Gray, Edwyn A. *Hitler's Battleships.* Annapolis, MD: U.S. Naval Institute, 1999.

Miller, D. M. O. *The Illustrated Directory of Warships.* Osceola, WI: Motorbooks International, 2001.

Roberts, John Arthur. *Battlecruisers.* Annapolis, MD: U.S. Naval Institute, 1998.

Tomajczyk, Stepen F. *Modern U.S. Navy Destroyers.* Osceola, WI: Motorbooks International, 2001

Canadian Navy <http://www.navy.dnd.ca>
Center of Military History <http://www.army.mil/cmh-pg>
Maritime National Park Association <http://www.maritime.org>
U.S. Marine Corps <http://www.usmc.mil>
U.S. Navy <http://www.navy.mil>
Warships of the World <http://www.warships1.com>

Places to Visit

You can see examples of some of the warships and related hardware contained in this book by visiting the naval and maritime museums listed here.

Arizona Memorial, Pearl Harbor, Honolulu, Hawaii <www.nps.gov/usar/>
Baltimore Maritime Museum, Baltimore, Maryland <www.baltomaritimemuseum.org>
Battleship Cove, Fall River, Massachusetts <www.battleshipcove.org>
Battleship *New Jersey*, Camden, New Jersey <www.bb62museum.org/whereto.html>
Battleship *North Carolina,* Wilmington, North Carolina <www.battleshipnc.com>
Boston National Historical Park, Boston, Massachusetts <www.nps.gov/bost/>
Canadian War Museum. Ottawa, Ontario, Canada <www.civilization.ca/cwm/cwme.asp>
Great Lakes Naval Memorial & Museum, Muskegon, Michigan <www.silversides.org>
Hampton Roads Naval Museum, Norfolk, Virginia <www.hrnm.navy.mil/>
Independence Seaport Museum, Philadelphia, Pennsylvania <http://seaport.philly.com>
Intrepid Sea-Air-Space Museum, New York, New York <www.intrepidmuseum.org>
Louisiana Naval War Memorial, Baton Rouge, Louisiana <www.usskidd.com>
Maritime Command Museum, Halifax, Nova Scotia, Canada
    <www.pspmembers.com/marcommuseum/>
National Museum of Naval Aviation, Pensacola, Florida <www.naval-air.org>
New Jersey Naval Museum, Hackensack, New Jersey <www.njnm.com>
San Diego Maritime Museum, San Diego, California <www.sdmaritime.com>
U.S. Naval Academy Museum, Annapolis, Maryland <www.usna.edu/museum>
USS *Saratoga* Museum Foundation, Providence, Rhode Island <www.saratogamuseum.org>
Vallejo Naval and Historical Museum, Vallejo, California <www.vallejomuseum.org>
Virginia War Museum, Newport News, Virginia <www.warmuseum.org>
Washington Navy Yard Museum, Washington, D.C.
    <www.history.navy.mil/branches/nhcorg8.htm>

Index

Picture Sources